A SERIES IN
NATURE

Also co-authored by Robert B. Warren:
Naked Spheres Of Ink

Oder this book online at www.classicartisticphotos.com or email bwarrengoodyear@aol.com

Most Trafford titles are also available at major online book retailers.

 www.trafford.com

North America & international
toll-free: 844 688 6899 (USA & Canada)
fax: 812 355 4082

Our mission is to efficiently provide the world's finest, most comprehensive book publishing service, enabling every author to experience success. To find out how to publish your book, your way, and have it available worldwide, visit us online at www.trafford.com

ISBN: 978-1-4269-4594-6

Library of Congress Control Number: 2010916835

Print information available on the last page.

Trafford rev. 03/23/2024

A SERIES IN

NATURE

By
Robert B. Warren

Trafford Publishing
1663 Liberty Drive
Bloomington, In 47403

To my Mom, Dad and the mystics of all Religions

In our beginnings are our ends and in our ends are our beginnings.
T.S. Elliot

"In Memory of John Baca Jr."

Preface

These photos are the result of 6 years of photographing while traveling between Washington state & Arizona. The insight behind these photographs goes back at least to my years of college in California, Washington & Hawaii. I say this because these are the years when my mind opened to the wonder, complexity and intricacies of the relationships between land, water, fire and air. While much has been forgotten it still remains and can be rediscovered through education, observation and effort.

While it is true that one can learn a lot by staying in one place for a long time, it is also true that one can learn a lot by traveling. This reflects one aspect of duality in nature.

I present these photographs in hopes that in seeing them they might make you the viewer happier and that they might also inspire you to see for yourself the myriad of wonders visible on our third planet from the sun.

Robert B. Warren

Acknowledgments

Thanks to all my teachers, especially those who I least appreciated

TABLE OF CONTENTS

Tree sap, Wallingford, WA

Rhubarb, Wallingford

Wallingford

Wallingford

Issaquah Highlands

Issaquah Highlands

Sunset, Issaquah Highlands

Sunset, Issaquah Highlands

Tree, Greenlake

S kagit valley tulips

Skagit valley tulips

Skagit valley tulips

Skagit valley tulips

Skagit valley tulips

Skagit valley tulips

Skagit valley tulips

Skagit valley tulips

Skagit valley tulips

Skagit valley tulips

Madrona tree, U.W. campus

Pastoral scene, Snoqualmie valley

Pumpkin field, Fall City

Mouth of the Nisqually River

Long Beach, Washington

Moclips Beach, WA

Moclips, WA

Moclips, WA

Mount St. Helens

Eastern WA

Northern Idaho

Montana

Montana

Yellowstone National Park

Yellowstone National Park

Yellowstone National Park

Yellowstone National Park

Yellowstone National Park

Yellowstone National Park

Yellowstone National Park

Yellowstone National Park

Yellowstone National Park

Yellowstone National Park

Yellowstone National Park

Yellowstone National Park

Yellowstone National Park

Aereol view, Western Oregon

Oregon coast

Oregon coast

Mt. Shasta, Northern California

Mt. Shasta, Northern California

View from 35,00 ft., Western U.S.

Sunset, Phoenix, AZ

Sunset, Phoenix, AZ

White Tanks Mountain Park

Flowers, Phoenix, AZ

Flowers, Phoenix, AZ

Desert Botanical Gardens

Desert Botanical Gardens

White Tanks Mountain Park

63

Grand Canyon

SF peaks, Northern AZ

Northern AZ

Indian Painted Desert

Indian Painted Desert

Indian Painted Desert

Salt River Canyon

Salt River Canyon

Salt River Canyon

Saguaro National Park

Saguaro National Park

Saguaro National Park

Saguaro National Park

Saguaro National Park

Saguaro National Park

Saguaro National Park

Twilight Saguaro National Park

Twilight Saguaro National Park

Moonrise, Saguaro National Park

Las Vegas

Chihuli chandelier, Bellagio hotel

Printed in the United States
by Baker & Taylor Publisher Services